How to Discover Your Family History

How to Discover Your Family History

How to Discover Your Family History

Contents

- Why You Need To Explore Your Past 9
- Genealogy And History 11
- Research And Effort Methods 13
- Creating A Family Tree 15
- Hiring A Professional 17
- Family Tree Software 18
- Getting Started In Genealogy 19
- Your Family: A Great Source For Genealogy Research 20
- Finding Sources For Genealogy Research 21
- Taking Genealogy Research Further 22
- Preserving Your Genealogy Research 23
- Canadian Genealogy: Knowing About Your Canadian Roots 24
- Society, History, Genealogy: Great Ancestry Research Sources In The Net 26
- Family Genealogy: Finding Out About Your Family's Past 28
- Tracing One's Roots Via Family History Genealogy 30
- Tips To Create Your Own Free Genealogy Site 32
- Five Key Genealogy Factors To Trace Your Lineage 35
- Tips On Choosing The Best Genealogy Testing Company In Canada 38
- Hone Your Research Skills With Genealogy Online For Dummies 41
- Genealogy Research: Unveiling The Past 43
- Genealogy Software: Tips On Finding The Right One 47
- Mormon Family History Center: Helping You Track Your Genealogy 50
- Mormon Genealogy: Finding Record Through The Family History Center 52
- Visiting A Family History Center 53
- Some Useful Genealogy Resources In Newfoundland 54
- Sawrey Genealogy: A Peek At The Rich Histoy Of The Sawrey Name 56
- Finding Your Roots: African American Genealogy 58
- Free Genealogy Database: A Great Way To Find Out About Your Ancestors 61
- German Genealogy: Finding Your German Ancestors 63
- Make The Best Use Of Genealogy Websites 65
- The Family History Library And International Genealogical Index 67
- How Important Is Genealogy 69
- Mormon Church Genealogy: Knowing About The History Of Mormons 71

Steps On Finding Free Genealogy Information 73
The Family Tree 75
Role Of Dna Testing In Genealogy Research 77

Why You Need To Explore Your Past

It seems simple to understand why history is important. There are countless times that history repeats itself. We are face with the same choices that we were just a handful of years ago. Did we learn from our mistakes or will we make the same ones over and over again?

Whether you believe in a Higher Power or not, there is still the question of what could have happened to those that are in your past. After all, don't you want to know who was in your family tree?

Could you be the descendant of one of the Kings or Queens of England? Perhaps you have an ancestor that was a war hero in the Revolutionary War. Perhaps the past isn't as pretty with ancestors that died in famines, illnesses or strife, only to save their children that you would eventually come from.

The "what if" type questions are out there and people in general are curious about what it means for them. If you want to know what your chances of learning more about your past you have to give genealogy a chance. You have to try to learn more.

The good news is that it's quite possible for many people to learn more about those in their family trees. The quest starts with understanding the process of genealogy and then learning how to get started on your own journey to learn as much as you can about those that have come before you in your family tree.

Genealogy is the study of family ancestry. It is the study and tracing of the family's pedigrees. During the process of genealogy, you will collect the names of your relatives, including those that are deceased and will then establish their relationship to each other.

This will include exploring various levels of your family tree as well including primary and secondary family members. You will use both documentation and word of mouth to help you to develop your family tree. The goal is to ultimately build a family tree that includes all of your relatives as far back as you would like to take it, or at least as far as you can take it.

How To Uncover Your Genealogy

Getting a family history of your family is a bit different. In genealogy, you technically only will get the names of your family members, creating a tree.

But, with a family history, you will take this one step farther by including information about each of those people. Learning more about the lives they lived is part of getting your family history.

Sometimes, this can be done at the same time as creating a family tree, other times it is a bit more complex because of how difficult it can be to learn this information. The goal is to gather as much information about your ancestors as you can to better understand your family's history in both public and private life.

Genealogy And History

One important thing to consider is the fact that your ancestry is part of history. Even if you can't get through the search for your family as thoroughly as you would like to, chances are you will learn a great deal about history and the role that your family may have played in that history. It could be small but it could be something important or something significant.

Sometimes, a search for your family's relatives can lead to reunions, or meetings with others that you may not have known or haven't seen in years. When you explore this path, you may find that distant cousins can offer you information. Or, you may find that a fight in the family has lead to a certain area of your family being cut off from you, and it may help to bring you all back together.

In addition to this, you may find that your family was separated for reasons that could not be controlled by them. For example, perhaps a war caused your family to split up. Or, foster home and adoption may have pushed your family into various directions that you didn't know about.

The fact is; there are likely to be family secrets, hush hush memories and much more that you can uncover when you use genealogy as your tool to uncovering your family's history and behaviors.

Indeed, you are likely to bring your family closer together and to have a better understanding for each other. And, for many people this means piecing back together family traditions and revealing family secrets that should have been told long ago.

Genealogy is actually something that people have done for centuries, if not longer. The need to know about your past is a natural, human curiosity and for that there have been numerous different people that have strived to learn as much as they can about their past throughout history.

Generally speaking, though, genealogy was something that was only done in olden times for those that were of power. For example, it was important to trace the genealogy of nobles, kings, queens and emperors. Any ruler needed to have information that showed that he was the right ruler for the job. Genealogy was used to help determine who the righteous ruler in many cases was.

If you wanted to claim that you had the right to have wealth and power, then you had to show that your ancestry proved that you were worth it. Demonstrating that you were the rightful heir or the rightful ruler was no little task and only genealogy could make this happen.

On a side note, the coat of arms of a family in the times of royalty where often used to help determine family lineage. This is actually called heraldry. It is the ancestry of royalty that was used in the quartering of the coat of arms of a family.

In many cases, though, modern ancestry studies have shown that many of those that used these methods to "claim" their righteous place in royalty where actually not authentic. They were merely fabrications that didn't prove anything, really. The most notable of these, of course, are those kings, emperors or other rulers that used their ancestry to show how they were linked to gods and the founders of the civilization itself.

The fact is that genealogy is something that can only be traced through truth, and that is something that is in the eye of the beholder. While you can probably find documentation to support more modern claims of ancestry, going back quite far in time is difficult.

Nevertheless, it is a story that you can tell! Imagine begin able to say that your great, great, great grandfather was part of the Royal Family!

The search for answers, then, will start with the need for authentic answers. For that, we turn to modern methods of uncovering the truth of families, first.

Research And Effort Methods

The process of learning about your family is likely to be one that offers several key searches. You'll use a wide range of these methods to get to the answers you need.

Types of relationships among your family members will include kinship to various groups or associations.

A surname search is called a one name study which will only give you details about a certain family name, passed down over time.

A small community, village or even church parish may offer help in the research methods. This also includes a one place study, which is just a search of on location's family lines.

Or, you can use a particular person to search for, for example trying to use your family's history to connect to another person's family.

The truth is that you'll likely need to go through many of these methods to find the answers that you need. In many ways, it's a process of looking where you didn't know you needed to look for answers regarding your family.

Even if your family doesn't have any known connection to the Church of Jesus Christ of Latter Day Saints, commonly known as LDS, you may still be able to use their records to help you to learn about your family.

During the 1900's, this group worked hard to create a program of moving all of their available records on ancestry into the valuable tool of microfilm. They placed all records they had in this medium, to safeguard them. In addition to this, they also created an index that was used to keep track of all of their members.

These two undertakings were large, thorough and would become one of the best tools for genealogical searches today. Today, these two projects have been folded together and are in two databases that are readily accessible.

How To Uncover Your Genealogy

The International Genealogical Index, which is known as IGI, is a tool that can be used. It is a transcription record of filmed civil and ecclesiastic records. These records have come from various locations from cooperating local areas around the world.

The other database that you can use is known as the Ancestral File or just simply AF. This database is used to collect the information about the member's contributions over time.

So, how can these databases help you? First off, the IGI is one of the best records of old birth and marriage records from the LDS. It has records of those that have been born, died and married starting from well back to 1500. Most of this information is from the United States, Europe and Canada.

Generally, information regarding members has been able to reveal quite a bit about family ancestry from these resources.

How can you use the LDS's collection of information? In Salt Lake City, Utah the collection of these microfilms is located. The resources are located at the Family History Library which has a vast collection of information regarding the entire society.

Yet, you don't have to travel there to find them. There are branches (some 4000 of them) around the country and world that can offer you help.

You can visit these locations, request information or even rent information for your on site research needs. In fact, they have expanded this search ability to the internet as well. You can visit the collection at this location at FamilySearch.org.

Creating A Family Tree

You have two options. First off, you can use just paper and your notes to create your family tree, which will look like a tree with all of its branches. But, this is hard to keep organized and can be a good tool if it is used correctly and managed.

The other option that you have is Family Tree Software products which can help you to determine an effective, electronic method of managing your family tree. In a later chapter we will talk more about how software can aid you in the process of uncovering your family tree. It's important, though to consider it as a tool for organization if not for finding your family members.

Placing the names of those people that you have learned about on your family tree is a process that requires a good eraser. It will be fun to put the pieces together, but it will also be difficult to organize.

Tips For Managing Your Family Tree

These tips will help you to get your family tree up and running. Your goal is to do the best that you can to keep it organized, so that it is easy for you to use later.

Group each person by the family that they belong to. If they have more than one connection, place these families near each other, and show their relation.

Group families by how they are related. If the two men are brothers, note this. Determine how each family relates to each other and note it.

Sometimes, using index cards can help you to keep large families organized. Even for those that are alive, create an immediate family index card, which includes the family, members, dates of birth and location that you can refer to later, over and over again.

Place blank spots near those people that you haven't found. For example, if you find out that there's a sister to one of your cousins that you don't know their name, mark that there is a sister. Later you may find their name and information.

How To Uncover Your Genealogy

Every once in a while, go back to the beginning of the project and see if there are any blanks that you can fill in. Often, you can learn a lot without realizing it.

It also pays to include others in this information that you've found. For example, if you are working on your genealogy project with your sister or aunt, when they see your family tree laid out, they may remember some additional information from the information that you have gathered. This information is important to gather.

Hiring A Professional

Probably the most expensive option for you to use is that of hiring a professional genealogist. These individuals are likely to provide you with the highest quality results, if you select one that is responsible, experienced and dedicated to providing the information to you.

Hiring a professional to do this work for you is a good idea, especially if you find yourself at a road block. Yet, it is essential that you do your homework to find someone that is willing and capable of providing you with the information that you need. There are, unfortunately, many organizations that are only looking for a payday rather than looking to help you to put together your family's story.

Find out what history that professional offers. What has he done for others? What is the farthest back he or she has been able to go for other families? In addition to this, you want to know how it will happen. Where will they gather additional information, how will they do more than you did and what can you expect to learn from what you are offering them?

In getting this information, you should also make sure that the professional will be providing you with an accurate family tree. For example, it makes no benefit to you to be filled with inaccurate information, and since you likely have no way of knowing if it's authentic, you need an upfront guarantee.

Getting references for those that you employ and then understanding what they really can offer you is essential. Make sure to check them out with the Better Business Bureau or similar organizations as well.

Family Tree Software

There are two types of genealogical software that you can purchase. By far the most is that which will help you to store, organize and later display the family tree information that you determine. This type of software is a benefit especially when a paper like tree would be too much to keep organized.

The other type of software available is that which can help you to find your family tree members. Some of this family tree software is only basic in what it can offer, some is much more thorough. Although not nearly as beneficial as using a professional genealogist, this software can help to point you in the right direction and help you to fill your tree in.

When selecting software for your use with your family tree project, realize that not all software is the same in quality. One of the best things you can do is to look for reviews of specific programs from the web and from other consumers that have used it. This will give you the best estimate of the quality and the worth of the software to you.

Using additional resources for your family tree search is important to those that want to go as far as they can with their search. Not only will it help to do this, but these tools can make organizing and time management of this large project much easier on you.

Getting Started In Genealogy

The study of genealogy is one that many people find quite rewarding. By taking the time to learn about their family, people often learn quite a bit about themselves in the process. Taking the time research your family can be quite a rewarding experience for you and for all that are around you. It will open the door to what your family has lived through and provide you with a look into the world that they were exposed to. Often, you will learn things that you may not have known about any other way.

To get started, you can easily take the time to learn about the options that are available to you. Your first decision will be how much work you will want to do on your own. For some, this may be taking the time to secure information from your family. Or, you may determine that you will want to work with a professional genealogist. Whichever your choice is, you should then pursue the options that you have in it. Depending on how deep into your past you would like to go, you have resources to help you to achieve these objectives.

When it comes to learning about your family, there should be little that stops you from doing so. You have many resources available to you because, like you, there are thousands of people that are dedicated to learning more about their family's history. It is a natural curiosity that many humans want to know. Where did they come from? And, when they do this, they can reap the rewards of learning more about themselves. Once you determine which way you will do this, you can move on to starting your task. More than likely, you will be like most others and find that this is a very rewarding experience to be in.

Your Family: A Great Source For Genealogy Research

One of the first things that you should do when you want to learn about your family's history is to begin by working on those living members of your family. Believe it or not, they may hold the keys that you need to learn about your family's history. Even though you may not think that it is important to talk to even your distant cousins, there are many benefits to doing so. Take into account what role that they play in your family's blood line and then begin talking to them about what they know about your genealogy.

The first thing that you will want to do is to work on names of ancestors. Some people may actually know the maiden names of female figures in your history. Some will know the names of those siblings and such that may not play a direct role in your history but still are part of your family tree. What you will want to do is to try to construct a family tree based on the names that have been given to you.

Don't stop there, though. You will want to hear the stories that they can offer you as well. These stories are full of a rich history and often have tidbits of history as well as tidbits of details that you need in order to make them come to life. You will find that these are things you need to know. Perhaps they will know the cities in which your family members grew up in. Or, they may know what region of the country their ancestors lived. They may know that someone was in the war or that someone else was in jail. These are informational pieces that you can use to begin your backward journey into your past. Each one of them offers a little more information about your past that you need to know.

Finding Sources For Genealogy Research

Once you begin working on your past, it is likely to become something that is amazingly interesting. Your first thing will be to talk to your family and friends to gather the information that you need. There is little doubt that this is the richest place to begin your search for your family's history. But, often, most people do not know what to do once they hit that fork in the road. What do they do once they get past the point of what their family can tell them? This is where you need to be as creative as you can be.

One thing you will want to do is to tap into the options that are offered to you on the web. For example, if you learn that your father's grandfather served in the military, you may be able to find information based on this on the web. You may be able to tap into old military records or even find information about something that he did heroically. Do this for all those that you have learned a little about. A little can provide much more down the road.

Once you begin researching the people that you have found, you may begin to stumble on information. If you find a grave marker, for example, you may be able to understand who this member's of your family's parents were. This will give you yet another piece in the puzzle. Going back through time can provide you with so much information like this. Small pieces begin to open up the puzzle of your genealogy. And, with each piece to the puzzle, you will likely become more and more intrigued by what it has to offer you. There are many ways that you can continue your search and it may be that information just seems to fall into your lap. Keep working at it and you will soon discover all that you need to know.

Taking Genealogy Research Further

Often people become discouraged when they have done all that they think that they can and can not seem to break their family's genealogy. This has happened to many because the road just runs cold. Not all families will have that warm history of stories that have been passed down. Some will not have much of a history in this manner at all. So, how do you take your search for your family further, then? There are several things that you can do including taking the time to explore the choices offered to you on the web.

One thing you may want to consider is using the internet's wide resources on your own. This may be doing this such as searching databases that are filled with valuable information. Some church organizations have a wide range of online databases to help you to track down your past relatives. This is part of their belief system. For others, there are many other resources including military information, war records and even just databases that may be filled with information about your family members because others out there are looking for information too. Tapping into any of these can be quite helpful.

If you still do not get the information that you need, consider using message boards, forums and even some genealogical blogs to help you. While they may not contain information about your family, they may provide you with good advice on finding people like this. You can also consider calling on a professional genealogical individual to help you in your search. This is often a way to go when you really are stuck and really want to pursue your family's history. Often, they can provide more information then you can simply because they have the necessary resources already set up to help you. The web is full of resources like this to further your investigation into your genealogy.

Preserving Your Genealogy Research

You have taken time to learn about your family. You have found a lot of valuable information. Perhaps you are still searching for additional information. Perhaps you will even keep doing this for several years. No matter what, you will want to be able to provide this information on to others that are in your family or even provide a safe place to store it as you go. In any case, there are some options that should be considered when it comes to preserving your family's genealogy. Doing so will help to keep it ready to be passed down or added to.

Probably the best way for you to do this is to secure the information in a genealogy software program. Not only can this program offer you a place to store all that is important to you that you have learned thus far, but it can also help you to find more solutions to your needs. For example, they may be able to point you in the right direction when it comes to looking for specific help with finding some information. Of course one of the biggest benefits to these programs is that they help to organize you so that you can easily move through your family's history and know what you are looking for.

Software programs that are designed for genealogy can also help you to pass on your information. In some cases, you will see that you can easily move your information from reports that are provided to providing it all in a book format that you can easily print off and have a hard copy to look at and even to share. You may find that these are some of the best tools to use when looking for your family even when it comes to tracking down them through a professional. Your genealogy means everything to you and you should provide the best preservation for it.

Canadian Genealogy: Knowing About Your Canadian Roots

People begin try to find information about their ancestors and about their family's past for different reasons. Some want to learn more about what makes them unique. Others want to construct a family tree. Some people have lost touch with once-dear relatives. Whole branches of their family may have drifted due to catastrophic historical events. Others need to know about past medical problems to solve mysterious illness common to their family.

Consider Canadians. Like people who live in the United States, their country is rich in culture and history, yet most everyone has immigrant roots. Unlike the United States, at least until recently, early immigrants to Canada came largely from France and Great Britain. If you are aware of ancestors in or from Canada and want to know more about them, you may want to hire a Canadian genealogist to help you in your quest.

No matter what the reason, it is easier today to find information than it ever was before the internet. Still, beginners may experience many barriers and slow-downs. Today, you can find many Canadian genealogists for hire who can help reduce frustration and get faster results in Canadian genealogical research.

They are well-informed about information sources, both on the internet and in hard-copy books and libraries. They are also experienced with the research process. They can help you develop a research plan, collect and organize documentation, and investigate Canadian genealogical research leads. Using a professional Canadian genealogist, you may even be able to secure original copies of some of your family's historical documents. You may even be able to take it a step further by finding out what happened to other branches of your family and locating distant relatives.

Learning about your personal history by gathering information and facts about your ancestors can be exciting, fun, and inspirational. Some people even learn they're related to famous historical figures. How many of us dreamed as kids that we are really a king or queen? Perhaps you'll learn that you are not entirely from one racial group. Maybe you'll be thrilled to find an unknown rich uncle somewhere up the family tree. You might even find a few horse-thieves or cattle-rustlers!

How To Uncover Your Genealogy

Certainly, you will learn about the circumstances and events that brought you to where you are today. You'll better understand the old family fears and hope handed down through generations. You'll pick up new stories to share at family gatherings. You may even get others in your family interested enough to join the search. There's something about learning your own unique heritage that makes you feel more grounded on this planet. And it certainly helps you bond with current relatives and previously-unknown cousins.

There's no telling what surprises you're likely to discover when you research your Canadian ancestry. If you're anxious to get started and learn, you must prepare to invest a lot of time and effort searching through Canadian databases, libraries, and public records. One choice discovery will open new paths for research. And your return will likely reflect your personal investment and commitment. And because it could take many years to track down everything you want to know, you may want to secure the services of a professional Canadian genealogist who can make that journey easier and overcome some of the common barriers in genealogical research. In genealogy, patience is a true virtue, and persistence is essential.

Society, History, Genealogy: Great Ancestry Research Sources In The Net

If families are the foundation of society, ancestry is the foundation of modern life. Many modern people want to better understand their history and the family that created them. Learning about your family and ancestry is great fun. People are frequently surprised at the interesting bits of genealogical gold they pick up along the way. You never know who you're related to until you dig into your ancestry. North Americans frequently learn that they carry the blood of the Lakota Sioux, the Cherokee, or the Navajo Nations in their veins.

The advent of modern technology and the internet has opened a new world for genealogical research. Although it can be challenging, time-consuming, and frustrating, tracing your family's ancestry and history is an extremely rewarding pursuit. Yes, you'll run into dead ends and lengthy delays, but you'll learn more about your family and your culture than you ever dreamed possible. You may even find relatives and life-long relationships that were impossible without the effort.

There are many websites that specialize in genealogy today, and you can use one or several of them to seek family ties and relations. One of these is the Culture Genealogy Society website, where you'll find links to respected, reputable information on families in different cultures and countries. There are sites that focus on Native American DNA genealogy, and European-based sites where you can find centuries-old information on your ancestors' lives and times.

The Culture Genealogy Society website provides copies of original documents for review, and it will give you a virtual family tree to help you track individuals and relationships over time. Other websites with information that's searchable by beginners also offer the help and experience of professional genealogists.

The time you spend searching for details about your family's past will produce much entertainment and some big surprises. For example, one genealogist undertook research on the ancestry of President George Bush, only to learn that he shares common ancestors with political rival John Kerry and, even more surprising, with infamous playboy Hugh Hefner! You never know what you'll turn up - an illegitimate son who spawned the grandfather of a famous preacher, a distant uncle who was hung as a horse-thief, perhaps even kings and queens. You may find that you are a mix of races or ethnic groups who've battled each other throughout history. Or maybe you'll find someone who first stepped on Plymouth Rock or who bought the first slave in America.

You simply won't know if you don't take the time to track down your family's heroes and villains. You could well find enough information to write a best-seller or assemble a family heirloom that will be cherished by generations to come. At the very least, you'll have a much better sense of who you are and where you came from by doing a little research into your unique ancestry.

Family Genealogy: Finding Out About Your Family's Past

Today, over 6.5 billion call planet Earth home, and our population is growing at a rate that was inconceivable even 100 years ago. One thing has not changed. No matter what era, no matter where, family is the basic building block of human society. No matter who you are, where you live, or what you do, your family history - including those long-gone ancestors - makes you what you are. A popular saying applies: history is destiny. In a way, family history is personal destiny.

Primitive man banded together in families to procreate and survive. These families were the base from which all civilizations sprang. Scientists claim to be able to trace all of mankind back to one mother. In a very real sense, we are all related.

Today's busy, largely urban societies seem worlds away from that past. It's easy to feel alone and isolated. Family units have shrunk from larger groups with grandparents, aunts and uncles, and cousins to what we call the nuclear family - mom, dad, and the kids. And in countries like the United States, Canada, and Australia where immigration built modern populations, families are even more separated from their traditional routes.

One way to get the information you need to discover your family's history is by conducting genealogical research. Searching back through historical records may lead you to discover that you are the descendant of kings - or thieves. One genealogist's study of famous people led to the surprising fact that President George Bush, rival Democrat John Kerry, and infamous playboy Hugh Hefner come, at some point in the past, from the same roots.

Genealogical research can change the way you see yourself. Perhaps you find people of different races or ethnicities in your family tree. Or maybe there's a famous political or cultural leader in your genetic past. Many Americans learn that their ancestors came from many different cultures and races, making their family a true American melting-pot.

Genealogical research can be a difficult, time-consuming, and lengthy project. But it's something that, once begun, entire extended families can participate in. As different relatives gather information, you can collect an interesting and exciting saga that you can then pass down to coming generations.

How To Uncover Your Genealogy

One of the most basic starting points is searching vital records. Many European countries have saved records of births, marriages, and deaths for centuries. Records of other life events like purchases of land, news-making dramas, and cemetery plot records are a great source of information.

The internet has produced an explosion in the amount and availability of information to help even the novice genealogist. There are many websites with tips, data, and services that can help you learn more about your family's history. There are also a number of reference sources and guides to help you in your journey.

Imagine how you'd feel to discover you're a descendant of Henry VIII, Louis IV of France, or Catherine the Great. Then think of the possibilities to learn you are a distant niece or nephew of Jesse James, Vlad the Impaler, Rasputin, Genghis Kahn, or Oliver Cromwell. Not everyone will have a famous hero or villain in their past, but the chances are good that you will.

So why not start that journey of discovery into your family's past by rummaging through some old documents or visiting the public library to see what you can find? You're going to run into some dead ends, be hung up by delays, and make mistakes. But that's part of genealogical research. You can be a kind of family history Indiana Jones searching the world for precious gems of information about the people who created you and shaped your destiny.

One thing you can count on is that you'll learn things you never imagined about your family history, and you'll have hours of interesting conversations with family members who are enthralled with your tales. Family history and genealogy brings long-separated relatives back together across time and space and helps us feel more grounded in a busy, crowded modern world.

Tracing One's Roots Via Family History Genealogy

The family has always been the basic building block of society. From the dawn of man, families have been the foundation of civilization. Family history defines the society, and the strength of families defines the rise and fall of every group and community. No matter what culture, no matter what era, the family history plays a critical role in unifying people and nations. In today's bustling urban environments where the boundaries of communication are quickly disappearing, the family continues to be the first and most basic part of human life. Family is the starting point upon which happy, productive, and stable lives are built.

Modern life in developed nations is characterized by individualism, and eccentricity is the style of the age. And it often seems that people are preoccupied with tomorrow's battles, not yesterday's successes. You might think that today's generations are less concerned than were their predecessors about their origins and where they come from. Ironically, however, interest in the search for our roots is growing rapidly. Learning about our family history - our genealogy - is getting more and more attention.

Webster defines genealogy as an account of the descent of a person, family, or group from an ancestor or from older forms or the study of family pedigrees. Genealogy is the science of family relationships, tracing an individual's family history and relatives, whether dead or alive, from the past into the present. Every person has their own reasons for searching through their past.

Some people may want to find a relative who has been lost to them for reasons beyond their control. For example, people involved in World War II who were forced from their homes may have lost most of their families. Many moved to other countries, and the location of their families was lost to time. Seeking out relatives after such a traumatic experience is healing.

Others, believing they are related to someone of historical note or influence, may be motivated by power or prestige. Or perhaps they were separated from parents or siblings due to family hardships.

No matter what the reason, genealogy is the search for one's personal history. That search can be as simple as gathering the names of relations and constructing a family tree that shows the family's branches and members. The search can be as exhaustive as researching and documenting the personal lives and experiences of family members. Many people create books that tell their family's history, creating a legacy for future generations.

Modern technology has created tools that make family history genealogy easier, more interesting, and exciting. It has opened a door for people who are serious about their research into family history. Recent discoveries about heredity and DNA have made it possible for people to scientifically identify those who share common ancestry.

Internet databases and websites have made it easy to find information about specific people by researching a few simple facts about them - where they've lived, names they've used, education, and a host of personal data. There are even computer programs designed specifically to help people research their family history genealogy.

Searching out your family and its history can be interesting and exciting. It's easy to start. Just talk to your relatives and harvest their memories. It's like a treasure hunt that leads you to unknown and exotic places. Your search into your family's past will introduce you to heroes and villains you never knew existed. Family history genealogy is the most personal adventure you'll ever undertake!

Tips To Create Your Own Free Genealogy Site

The internet is a rich information source, used by people every day for casual browsing and for serious research. Today, genealogical research is fast becoming a major web category.

Genealogy is the study of family relationships through time. It's most well-know product is the family tree. Undertaking genealogical research involves extensive research, careful documentation and verification, and presentation of findings. It is a time-consuming, sometimes frustrating, project with invaluable rewards.

If you're interested or involved in your own genealogical research, you may want to consider creating your own family genealogy website. There are some important reasons for doing this. It helps you document what you've learned. It also gives easy access to family members and may stimulate their contribution to or participation in your research. The most important reason: it's fun!

You can also find tools and advice on family genealogy research on the internet. There are many websites devoted to the topic, and they offer not only help and advice but raw information in the form of searchable databases.

You can find software programs designed for genealogy research as well. These programs make it easier to gather information, organize and interpret your data, and create documents (like family trees and narratives) to record your family's history. Genealogy software can automate processes like submitting your GEDCOM file to several sites at once, allowing you to make more effective use of your time and reach more information sources.

You don't have to wait until your research is finished to start your family genealogy website. As mentioned, it may help you gather more information, filling in missing pieces of the puzzle, to make it freely available to the public. And you don't have to pay a lot of money to own your own website. Services like Yahoo GeoCities offer free services and hosting at a nominal price. However, if you're a newbie to the internet, you may want to use a more comprehensive service like Site Build It! to make the web authorship tasks easier and focus on your research.

How To Uncover Your Genealogy

Once you decide where and how to manage your family genealogy website, you'll need to decide on some details: site design, content writing, copyrights, and access rights. You'll have to purchase your own domain name, and you can find out what names are and are not available by querying a who is service. You can own a domain name for a small fee: the costs comes in finding a host server. In developing pages, you can use your own HTML editor like the popular Macromedia Dreamweaver or Microsoft's FrontPage. If HTML and coding aren't your thing, you can buy those services at a reasonable price by visiting some of the "freelance" websites. Be careful, though, to assure your provider is experienced, dependable, and honest.

When you decide to build your website, you should consider these elements:

* You may want to use an easy-to-remember, catchy website name. Since it's your family's name and information, you should ask them about their preferences and opinions.

* For a better chance of being included on search engine results, your heading, URL, and first paragraph must contain the surnames of family branches you've identified. Use these names several times in your content. Try also to use words and forms of words related to family genealogy like "family tree," "family history," "ancestors," or "genealogy."

* The quality of your content is important for several reasons. First, you'll want to offer interesting easy-to-read information. You'll also want to be sure visitors to your website can find what they need easily. Your home page should contain several short paragraphs on your family's history and links to your second-level or detail pages, family photographs, and copies of records. We recommend that you limit the amount of graphics on your home page because they make the page take longer to open, and you'll lose visitors who don't have the patience for the page to download.

* Develop a good navigation system with plenty of text links and navigation buttons. Your links should make it very clear what the user will find when he clicks on them. Simple, clear titles are best.

* Using proper meta tags in your HTML code is important for search engines. If you want your website and home page to come up early in the list of searches, be sure to use your family name and keywords that are relevant to the story you're telling.

* In addition to including links to other genealogy websites, try to get them to link to you as well. You may be able to work out agreements with other sites for trading links, or you might consider joining a webring focused on your family or genealogy in general.

* Be sure to provide contact information on your website that is easy to see. Because you're doing research, you'll want to make it easy for your visitors to get additional family information to you. You'll also want to give them an easy way to contact you with questions or feedback on your website.

These are some basic tips on how to go about creating a family genealogy website that will both publicize your findings and bring in additional information. Your content can range from the specific and personal, concentrating on your family and its branches, to the general and educational, sharing your broader experiences with family genealogy.

Your family genealogy website will be a satisfying project that makes what you've learned about your family available to everyone. It will be a source of information, entertainment, and education that your whole family will appreciate. It will also be a wonderful tool for expanding and enhancing your family genealogy research effort.

Five Key Genealogy Factors To Trace Your Lineage

Genealogy is the study of family history and ancestors - also known as family lineage. It involves collecting the names of living and deceased relatives and establishing the relationships between them. Documenting important and incidental facts is also part of good genealogical research. A person who engages in this type of study is known as a genealogist, whether a professional or a hobbyist.

Genealogists who want to make a thorough study of the family and its ancestors must begin with and collect specific information if their project is to be successful. Here are some of the basic facts you'll need to know as you conduct your genealogical research.

Family Names

The family surname (last name) is a critical tool in genealogical research. It begins the search and helps identify family branches that may use different variations on the surname.

Normally, the family surname originated from a male family head, the village where the family lived, or the family occupation. For example, the MacDonald surname describes people who are descended from a man named Donald. The Sawrey family surname is the name of the village in England where they lived. The Taylor family surname describes what that family did to earn its living.

Your family lineage will also include completely different family names, reflecting the marriage of daughters important to your family history. These different names may be similar because they were neighbors in the same village or region. They may also be entirely different nationalities or ethnic groups, reflecting the mix of people through migration and intermarriage. And most U.S. immigrants adopted new surnames when they arrived at Ellis Island, either because their original surname was too hard to pronounce or the immigration official misspelled it!

Over time, as family's move to different locations, take on different dialects or languages, or have private reasons for making a change (escape from the law?), surnames evolve into different forms. The Clan MacDonald, for example, now also contains McDonalds, MacDonnells, and McConnell, to name just a few.

To find your ancestors' family name, try researching public records like birth, marriage, and death certificates. You might also try trade directories or census returns.

Places

Knowing where your ancestors lived is a basic part of learning about your lineage. Families migrate, split into branches, and build empires. To learn where your family has lived, you'll need to search vital records like census documents, records of land purchases and sales, court proceedings, and estate and probate records.

To avoid confusion, when you list a place name for a family member or branch, start with the smallest first. For example, list the village or town first, the county second, the province or state third, and the country last.

Given Names

Our earliest ancestors were often known by a single name (thus, the Clan MacDonald descends from Donald). Later, it became necessary to identify people in a family by a separate and unique name. Given names, or first names, are critical to genealogical research.

Given names help you identify accurate relationships between family members and tell something about the family's history. Many given names are, in fact, the surnames of other related families and branches. Given names can contain valuable hints about lineage.

For example, a son's first name may be in memory of a paternal or maternal grandfather. A daughter's first name may have been inherited from her grandmother. It has also been common to use the mother's maiden name as a given name.

Dates

Knowing when events happened is important to building a family tree or timeline. It's important to know when your ancestors were born, when they married, and when they died. Other important dates can enrich your family history and provide important information about the time they lived. The date of baptism, medical treatment, transfer of property, or even the date of a trial can add much to your genealogical research and provide more clues to follow.

Sources for dates important to your family could include vital records maintained by governments, church records, the family Bible, and personal documents like diaries and letters.

Occupation and Employment

What your ancestors did for a living is an important piece of information that will help your search and provide important context for better understanding your family's history. Historically, occupations were passed down from father to son. Some families adopted surnames that described their occupation or trade. Consider the surnames Tailor, Shepherd, Fisher, Baker, Clark (clerk), Chandler (candle maker), Bowman, and Seaman. A very common name, Smith, derives from the blacksmith occupation.

Good sources for information on occupation include city directories, trade membership lists, obituaries, and military service records.

When you embark on your study of you family's history and your ancestor, you should start with these five basic pieces of information. Now, go out there and do some great genealogy!

Tips On Choosing The Best Genealogy Testing Company In Canada

Modern science unlocked many secrets of human relationships when DNA analysis moved from university research to practical applications. Popularized by a multitude of TV programs, DNA testing and analysis solves crimes and established or disproved paternity. Study of the genetic information in our DNA to track father-to-son and mother-to-daughter evidence is still in its infancy, but progress is being made by scientists who call this research genetic genealogy.

Having your DNA analyzed can yield interesting results. Since Y-chromosome information transfers from father-to-son without change, genealogists can trace fathers' lineage for generations. Mitochondrial DNA passes from mothers to their children. It is believed that all people European descent can be traced back to one of eight women.

The areas of inquiry in genetic genealogy are paternal and maternal lines, biogeograhic and ethnic origin, and human migration. Genetic genealogy can't tell you much about individuals, but a sample of your DNA can tell you about the major family groups that are your ancestors. Basically, it can help you identify your ancestral homeland and prove or disprove biological relationships.

People living in Canada who are researching their family history and ancestry should understand the basics about DNA (deoxyribonucleic acid) and genetic genealogy if they want to know where they came from. As a first step in genealogical research, DNA testing and analysis can set broad parameters for identifying your ancestors.

But to get accurate results, you must select a reliable, accredited laboratory with expertise in genetic genealogy. Here are some guidelines to help assure you can trust the information you get from the laboratory you use.

1. Check the record and credentials of the laboratory. Does it claim to be expert in genetic genealogy? Does it follow standards set by the Standards Council of Canada? Is the lab accredited (or approved) by that group? This is perhaps the most important evidence that the laboratory you select adheres to consistent accepted practices.

2. Has the laboratory established a record or reputation in the area of genetic genealogy? DNA analysis supporting genealogical research doesn't look at the same area of DNA that criminologists use for solving crimes. Especially because genetic genealogy is in its early stages, your laboratory should be able to document substantial experience in Y-chromosome and mitochondrial DNA analysis.

3. Verify claimed experience by asking what markers the lab is using for genetic genealogy results. DNA analysis for tracing ancestry doesn't look at specific genes. Rather, it focuses on what is called non-coding Y-chromosome DNA. If you understand genes and genetic research, this information may be very helpful to you in assessing your laboratory.

4. Has the laboratory verified the accuracy of its procedures? A basic way laboratories establish credibility is to have different labs run the same test in the exact same way on different samples of the same genetic material. If results vary, there is something different in the procedures. Verification involves establishing that the equipment is accurate and properly calibrated, that lab staff follow the exact same steps, and that results are recorded accurately. Be sure the lab you use has validated its procedures in this way.

5. ISO (International Organization for Standardization) 17025 is the standard that testing and calibration laboratories use to establish that they meet common and accepted management and technical practices. In addition to showing equipment and procedures are standard, ISO 17025 established that the laboratory has a documented quality management system. It is important to know that your laboratory conforms to the international standard. When you choose an accredited DNA laboratory in connection with the internal control system, it ensures that the DNA testing as well as analysis is performed under an international recognized DNA laboratory protocols. This can give you more reliable and accurate results.

6. Ask the laboratory if it has a genealogy specialist who can explain the results to you clearly so that you understand the genetic testing results. If they don't have someone on staff who can fill that role, ask if they use a consulting service that can assist you.

7. Find out if the laboratory has access to and uses databases commonly used for genealogical research. This will greatly improve your ability to organize and interpret the information you receive.

Genealogical researchers in Canada should be sure they can rely on the results from their genetic genealogy laboratory. These are basic tests to assure your laboratory will produce accurate results to help you in your quest to learn about your ancestry.

Hone your Research Skills with Genealogy Online For Dummies

Learning about a person's ancestors, or genealogy, has long been a difficult challenge, even for people who do it for a living. But when the internet came along and information exploded, traditional genealogists found themselves joining the technology revolution.

Easier access to information about individuals and families has brought a flood of novices into the field of genealogical research. Even when they don't know how to go about doing the research, they are usually familiar with the technology - e-mail, web browsing, blogs, and the host of web opportunities available today. For those newcomers to genealogical research with a passion for technology, genealogy is a fascinating and rewarding pursuit.

The first obstacle is likely to be finding and following the information you need. It's hard to know which information and materials are going to pay off. It's easy to get discouraged as a novice genealogist, but don't give up. There's always a solution. All you have to do is learn more about the process.

"For Dummies" books have become very popular over the last several years, and they're dominating genealogical research today. "Genealogy Online" by April Leigh Helm and Matthew L. Helm is the latest offering, and it has five parts that are very helpful in helping you find your way to your family's history.

Useful for both beginners and pros, Parts 1 and 2 of "Genealogy Online" offer valuable tips for conducting genealogical research, including areas like ethnic research, geography, surnames, and government records.

But Part 4 is the most important and helpful part of this book. It contains information about:

- 10 leading genealogical publications available on the internet
- 10 guidelines on designing a genealogy webpage
- 10 ways to do productive, rewarding genealogical research
- Yellow pages with important genealogical websites and website descriptions

How To Uncover Your Genealogy

You'll get more out of your web searches and surfing when you use the section on search engines outlining great ways to better get information through robots and spiders. For example, a common mistake of beginners is to type the surname alone into a search engine. They're surprised when the get a lot of irrelevant responses that make it harder to find the important sites. Following the tips in "Online Genealogy" will help avoid this frustration.

The book is also available on CD, and this helps make best use of the variety of shareware and commercial programs, whether for Mac or Windows, and tools that genealogists use frequently. While you can't find everything you need on web sites or with computers, "Online Genealogy" gives helpful information on doing research the old-fashioned way with books.

Beginning genealogists give this book high marks, expressing gratitude for its focus on research planning and how to use a computer to do the work.

"Online Genealogy" offers a gem in pointing users to the Bureau of Land Management's database of land patents, inherited from the old General Land Office. Through that database, genealogists can find and download copies of early ancestor's old land patents.

Even experienced genealogists praise "Online Genealogy," reporting it helped them build new skills and improve their results in genealogical research. Citing better ways to preserve old photographs and notes, these seasoned pros also appreciated tips and strategies on planning travel for effective genealogical research.

Today, having "Online Genealogy" as a resource, beginners are dummies no more!

Genealogy Research: Unveiling The Past

The word genealogy derives from the Greek "genea," meaning family or race, or "genos" meaning race. It is the study of lineage, tracing family roots as far as possible into the past.

There was a time when your lineage dictated your place in life, your future, and your possibilities. In many parts of the world, this still holds true. In democratic societies, lineage may be important, but it does not dictate your future earnings or social position.

However, your ancestors bequeathed to you your genetic make-up and a history of events that do contribute a great deal to who you are.

Why should anyone want to attempt genealogical research?

Today's world is busy and crowded. It's easy to lose touch with your personal roots. Understanding your family's history helps you have a solid sense of who you are and where you're going. Genealogical research strengthens your sense of self in a world of relative strangers.

Genealogical research helps you re-connect with long-lost relatives, discover and form relationships with new ones, and bring your modern family together with a common purpose. Learning about your family's ancestors is a way to honor them and their contributions to your life.

Solving the mystery of your family's history helps you learn about important historical events that brought your family to where they are today. It lends understanding and appreciation for the hardships and victories that formed your family's values, hopes, and fears.

Genealogical research also turns up some very unexpected surprises. People learn about ancestors with colorful and interesting lives - from the illegitimate child who bore the father of royalty to the hero who saved a village to the villain who plundered it. People learn that their ancestry includes different races and combines different cultures. Some people even find long-lost rich uncles and vast inheritances!

In North America, where most people descend from immigrants, genealogical research helps you locate far-away family branches. There's no better reason to travel around the world than to meet "new" relatives, who are also a great source of interesting tales about your common ancestors.

Sometimes, genealogical research can turn up information to help you understand some rare and mysterious medical condition that seems to plague your family. What you learn might help you identify both genetic and environmental causes and solutions for the problem. In some cases, it might convince you to adopt rather than have your children naturally.

Many people have gathered enough interesting, entertaining information about their family to write a book, even a best-seller. Others keep it within the family and create an heirloom volume that future generations will cherish.

Okay. I want to learn about my ancestry. Where do I start?

Before you begin, you should know that genealogical research can be difficult, time-consuming, and frustrating. You'll run into dead-ends and go on wild goose chases. But the benefits well out-weigh the costs.

A good beginning for your genealogical research is to search through public records in communities where your family has lived. Local governments maintain records of births, marriages, and deaths as well as things like land sales and purchases. Local newspapers maintain archives where you can search for your family members' names.

Another early step should be interviewing the oldest family members. Get the names of their fathers, mothers, grandparents, aunts, uncles, and cousins. Perhaps more personally satisfying, listen to their memories and the stories they learned about your family from their oldest relatives. This should be an early step, as you can't know how long they will be around. And the information you gather from them will give you invaluable clues to follow later.

Conducting genealogical research, you become an investigator. You find clues you don't even know are clues until you learn that one fact that puts it together. You find friends of friends of friends that can help. Like Sherlock Holmes or a crime scene investigator, you find the evidence, analyze it, and track down more leads.

Using the internet as a source is both fun and profitable. You'll find many websites dedicated to genealogical research that not only give you access to national and international databases of surnames, family branches, and nationalities but that also offer tips and guides that will help you through your journey into the past. You can also find public records online that contain information in places you can't afford to travel.

Many families already have websites devoted to their line. Scottish clans, for example, already have a huge amount of research online. You may get lucky and find that a distant relative has already done much of the work for you.

The Church of Jesus Christ of Latter-day Saints offers free to the public access to its Family History Library in Salt Lake City, Utah, and over 3,000 Family History Centers in 64 countries worldwide. While established and maintained to help Mormons trace their ancestry, the information is available to everyone.

If you enjoy your research project, you'll probably want to join online communities of genealogical researchers like you. You can share your problems and find solutions that others have already used. You can get hints and tips on where and how to find information. You may even find a distant relative who's engaged in the same pursuit.

Most countries have organizations and associations devoted to genealogical research. Family History Societies and governmental agencies have archives and records about families in their country and information on migration patterns and times.

Genealogical research is an interesting, exciting project that will produce information about your family and your ancestors to enrich your life and your relationships. It often becomes a family project, bringing together relatives who hardly speak. The more you learn, the more you want to learn, and family friends will want to be part of the adventure.

On a personal level, genealogical research can enhance your sense of self, help you feel more grounded in this world, and give you a new perspective on your life and future. Think of your reaction at learning you're related to a famous political figure or, on the other hand, an infamous villain. You might even be in a line of kings!

You'll never know about your family history until you take that first step on your journey into the past.

Genealogy Software: Tips On Finding The Right One

Undertaking genealogy (the study of family history and ancestry) is an increasingly popular passion all over the world. Learning about your family's past - where they began, what happened to them, and what individual ancestors did - is a great way to enhance your sense of self, rebuild relationships with your relatives, and learn about fascinating events in history.

No matter why you choose to conduct family genealogy, you'll find genealogy software an excellent time-saving tool. Many different brands of genealogy software are available at comparable prices and features. They make it easier to find data, organize and analyze the information you've collected, and create documents that bring your findings together in an interesting, creative package. Most programs include the well-known family tree among features to help you create charts, maps, and narrative accounts of your family's history.

To find the genealogy software that best meets your needs, you'll need to do some research. For example, the 2008 Genealogy Software Review compares 10 different software packages on a number of factors including features, usability, reporting capability, and help and support. It also offers detailed narrative evaluations of each package. ConsumerSearch.com, a popular product review website, also evaluates five top software packages.

You'll also want to check out articles on genealogy research and genealogy software to learn from others' experience and help identify your unique interests and requirements. You'll be making an investment of personal time and money when you purchase genealogy software, so be sure you make the best personal choice by making an educated choice.

Whether you're a professional genealogist or an individual with a passion for your own family's history, the right genealogy software will make your work easier and more rewarding. It will cut down on the number of dead ends, delays, and barriers in your path, and it will save effort in compiling and presenting your findings.

One outstanding benefit of genealogy software is the range of products you can create to organize your work, document your research, and present your findings. For example, you may need an organized printable checklist of steps involved in genealogical research if you're a beginner. This will help you keep track of progress and avoid skipping over an important task.

You may want to generate ancestor charts that show the direct line of individual ancestors. Or you may want the ability to create narrative ancestor reports so that you can tell the story in a more entertaining way that you can share with others. Perhaps you'll want to produce an ancestor pedigree report, a graphic timeline showing people and events, or a comprehensive family chart that depicts whole family branches and their relationships.

Clearly, before you purchase genealogy software, you'll want to give careful thought to what you want and need to do to gather the information and how you'll want to assemble and present the information when you're done.

Here are some important criteria you should keep in mind as you assess genealogical software packages to find the one that best meets your needs:

* **Ease of use.** You'll want genealogy software that's user-friendly. Clear instructions, well laid-out navigation, and efficient data entry forms will save you much time and confusion.

* **Setup and installation.** Your genealogy software should be easy to download and install. It should have clear and simple instructions for installation. Your setup options should be logical and straightforward. And installation and setup steps should be clear and unambiguous to avoid frustrating confusion and errors that will haunt you later on. You'll also want to be sure that your computer equipment can handle the genealogy software. What type of operating system, processor speed, and graphics card are necessary to run the software without hang-ups and slow-downs.

* **Features.** How do you plan to use the genealogy software? You may want more features to help you conduct research and perform data searches, not caring so much about creating a family tree or graphics at the end of the research process. On the other hand, you may already have much of the information and data you plan to use. Perhaps you need software that will help you create attractive and interesting graphics, charts, maps, and narratives summarizing your findings.

* **Software support.** If you don't have a lot of experience with using software, you'll need a comprehensive help function including a detailed glossary, step-by-step instructions for specific

tasks, and a way to contact the company directly for answers for your questions and personal help with difficult tasks.

Modern technology has made the job of genealogical research an easier, more rewarding project. Genealogy software is valuable tool for getting the best possible results when you research your family's history and ancestry.

Mormon Family History Center: Helping You Track Your Genealogy

For years, the Family History Library created by the Church of Jesus Christ of Latter-Day Saints, more popularly known as the Mormons, have provided genealogical information to the public. The popular Library in Salt Lake City, Utah, has attracted genealogists from all over the world, though many have not been able to get there.

A genealogist in Sydney, Australia, had to travel almost 13,000 kilometers to search for information he didn't, in fact, find. Time-consuming, tiring, and expensive, he learned the hard way that getting there doesn't guarantee successful genealogical research.

Being aware of that dilemma, the Mormon's generously created 3,400 Family History Centers in 64 countries as branches of the larger Library. Today, there are almost 40 Family History Centers with traveling distance of our friend from Sydney.

Every month, the Family History Centers circulate hundreds of thousands of rolls of microfilmed records, together with books and other genealogical resources, so that genealogists no longer have to take the costly risk of traveling to the Library in Salt Lake City. The Centers are located in most major cities and in smaller communities worldwide.

Collectively, the Family History Centers maintain massive amounts of data of genealogical value including records on census, churches, vital statistics, probate, land, and immigration.

The Centers and their collections are available to the public at no cost, and they're staffed by knowledgeable volunteers from the Church and community. The volunteers eagerly provide help and answer questions to Center visitors. Because the Family History Centers are funded largely by Mormon congregations in the community, they are located in the Church buildings.

Known also as satellite libraries, the Family Health Centers provide genealogy-related documents and books, databases for family trees, maps, and specific family histories to their users. Most Family Health Centers contain large collections of books and series of microfilm and microfiche that can be reviewed anytime.

Frequently, the Family Health Center can not release the records that visitors ask for, since the records may still be of value to the Family History Library and other researchers.

However, it is possible to borrow materials for a small fee, ranging from $3 to $5 for each microfilm roll. Since the reference materials are normally in circulation throughout the network of Family Health Centers, it can take from two to five weeks for them to arrive at the place where you requested them. The Center will hold it there for your use for about three weeks, when it returns the materials to circulation.

If you're concerned that the Family Health Centers may be a pulpit or trap to convert people to the Mormon faith, don't be. The Church has made the Library and its services available to the general public for years because they believe that ancestry and family history are vitally important to today's families.

Their purpose is straightforward and honest, and they respect everyone's spiritual privacy. Rather, they are committed to encouraging and supporting family history genealogy as a important part of self-identity and family unity.

Mormon Genealogy: Finding Record Through The Family History Center

One organization stands out in the field of genealogical research: The Church of Jesus Christ of Latter-Day Saints (or LDS). Popularly known as the Mormon church, they have a special reason for needing genealogical information, what they call an ancestor's proxy baptism. Done since 1840 for people who have already passed away, a living person acts as a proxy who is baptized on behalf of the deceased. The practices is limited to this religious sect.

But to do ancestor proxy baptisms, Mormon genealogy efforts have been intense. This has resulted in the LDS having a huge database, the International Genealogical Index, or IGI, open to the general public through their Family Search website. The church also maintains a Central Library and Family History Centers in Salt Lake City, Utah.

Anyone can use these resources. LDS members contribute the biggest part Mormon genealogy records in the IGI. Starting with an easy-to-use data input form, database searches are based on a deceased individual's name, their parents' and spouse's names, date of birth, and location (worldwide) to search available records for relevant information. You can search with as little as the person's name and region. The IGI is basically a huge index of surnames recorded in the Mormon Family History Centers and website.

As you might guess, their FamilySearch.com website is biased in favor of church-member needs, but it contains many resources where you may find your own non-Mormon family members. Searches through the Mormon genealogy database can be cumbersome, though, because of the size and amount of detail the it contains.

Visiting A Family History Center

It's hard to name a genealogist who wouldn't want to visit the Mormon's famous Family History Library in Salt Lake City. But since travel to Salt Lake City was not always possible, the church opened more than 3400 Family History Centers in 64 countries. They provide over 100,000 rolls of microfilmed Mormon genealogy that circulate the Centers every month. Microfilm records contain vital, census, land, immigration, probate, and church records as well as other important genealogical information. In the United States, you can find Centers in both large cities and smaller communities.

Because they're funded largely through local congregations, they are usually located in church buildings. These satellite libraries that contain Mormon genealogy resources to help people in their genealogical research. Visitors can use the Family History Centers without charge. Volunteers are eager to help by answering questions and offering advice. Records may not be available at a specific Center because they're circulated through the system, but you can request a loan of specific records through a Center volunteer, paying from $3 to $5 per film.

It can take two to five weeks for the requested Mormon genealogy information to arrive a the local Center, and they'll be held there for about three weeks for the requester to pick them up. After three weeks, the Center will return the information to circulation.

Here are some tips on how specific record requests are handled:

• Requesters can renew the loan if they need more time.

• It is possible to have specific records permanently located at a specific Family Health Center by renewing the microfilm rolls twice or paying within three rental periods.

• To arrange a permanent loan, requesters should inform the Center of their intentions and pay the three rental periods in advance for the Mormon genealogy research information.

• While books can't be borrowed from the Centers, you can ask one of the Center's volunteers that they be microfilmed.

Some Useful Genealogy Resources In Newfoundland

Ancient Norsemen called it Vinland, but we know it as Newfoundland today. Settling on this largest of North American islands, the first settlers, known as Beothuk, probably migrated from nearby Labrador. Historians suggest that the next settlers after the Beothuk were what we now call Native Americans, in this case a tribe known as the Micmac.

If you have family there today or know of ancestors from Newfoundland, you'll be happy to know that there are several resources that are available for genealogical research in Newfoundland.

These government agencies and offices have documents and resources that may help you locate important information and get more details about your Newfoundland heritage:

Department of Government Services and Land

This department issues and maintains records of birth certificates, marriage licenses, and death records. The department's services are located throughout the island, and you can get application forms to obtain records related to your ancestors there. .

Provincial Archives

Records documenting historical events and data are housed in the Provincial Archives. They maintain church records that include baptism, marriage, and internment certificates. You may also be able to find these same records from the vital statistics register.

Public Library

Although there are community libraries throughout the island, the capital and largest city, St John's, is served by three major public libraries that maintain important historical records and documents. All of these offer free internet access.

* A C Hunter Public Library in the Arts & Culture Centre, also the Provincial Resource Library, supports all of the province's other libraries
* Marjorie Mews Public Library on Torbay Road serves the city's north-east end

* Michael Donovan Public Library, in Waterford Valley Mall, services St. John's west end

Non-Governmental Resources

In addition to government resources, several Newfoundland groups and associations are organized help people with their genealogical research. They include:

* Association of Newfoundland and Labrador Archives (ANLA), located in St. John's, has a well-kept archive of province records. In addition to keeping the records, the ANLA administers and promotes education programs through training and workshops.

* The Newfoundland Historical Society is reputed to be the first heritage association in the province. Seeking to promote knowledge and public discussion, the Society is supported by membership fees, donations, and publication sales. It sponsors a series of free public lectures in the fall and spring and publishes books and bibliographies on Newfoundland and Labrador history that may be helpful in genealogical research.

Other helpful associations in Newfoundland that you can contact for your search are the Bay St. George Heritage Association in Stephenville, the Ferryland Historical Society in Ferryland, and the Alberta Family Histories Society. Newfoundland's Grand Banks website was constructed to support genealogical research on Newfoundland. Open to all, visitors should find fundamental genealogical and historical data for the province. Of course, it will be important to consult directories and visit churches and cemeteries on the island to do thorough research in Newfoundland.

The internet is an excellent tool for learning more about Newfoundland ancestry and family history. Using almost any dependable search engine, you can find several Newfoundland genealogy-related websites that offer inexpensive, even free, information.

Sawrey Genealogy: A Peek At The Rich Histoy Of The Sawrey Name

There's only one thing in this world no one can take away from you - only one thing you truly own. That unique thing is you - the person you are - the sum of your body, your thoughts and emotions, your experience, and your past, present, and future. These things make you different from every other human being in this crowded world. Your identity and the person you are belong to you, no one else.

Yet who you are is largely determined by your history, both in your personal experience and in your genetic history. Who you are reflects your ancestors, the kind of lives they lived, the conditions of their time, and their experiences. Whether you influenced personal traits through genetic inheritance or stories passed down through generations, your history is uniquely yours as well.

Have you ever wondered about your past - your family's roots and history? If you have, you'll find genealogy an interesting and rewarding pursuit. Genealogy is a study of human relationship, the search for one's kin. Looking back and time to find your bloodline, learning about people previously unknown, and meeting relatives you never knew about can be exciting and interesting. In finding out more about your family's history, you'll learn about yourself.

Every single name has its own unique heritage. The science of genealogy pulls back the curtain and sheds light on the mystery behind every name.

For example, the surname "Sawrey" can be traced back more than 13 centuries across many countries. Known before the 8th Century, this Norse or Viking surname was adopted and modified by many generations from different cultures.

Originally the name for a village, Sawrey described a fallow marsh in England. Over time, the village name was used by people to identify themselves. With population growth and development, Sawrey family members carried the name with them on their travels throughout northern England and Wales. With the different languages, dialects, and accents in Middle Age England, the name took on different spellings and pronunciations. Today, people named Sowraie and Sowrah are members of the Sawrey family.

How To Uncover Your Genealogy

It's impossible to predict what you'll learn about your family's history when you begin to do genealogical research. Who knows, you might even by a Sawrey! Or you may find that your family's roots go back even further into history than the 8th Century.

Learning about your parents' parents' parents' ... etc. ... brings a great sense of belonging and identity in a modern world where people are often isolated and lonely. Family history brings people back together in the joy of discovery on a very personal level. And the things you learn will be valuable information to give following generations a sense of stability and personal definition.

There are few things as rewarding as being able to tell the story of your family's journey through time. This is an invitation to join the quest and do some genealogical research into your own history.

Finding Your Roots: African American Genealogy

Yes, we are indeed talking about learning or re-discovering your lineage, family history and any links with possibly famous personalities by looking up your African-American Genealogy information by consulting the elders in your family – or you can do it online! Whichever way you choose to go about finding out more about your African-American past, if you are dedicated enough and research in an organized manner, you are sure to be able to reconnect with your roots, in an enjoyable manner – and who knows, even collect enough matter to make up your own family tree!

The convenience and comfort of your own home or office can be the best place for you to get on the net and recreate some of your family's past by using latest web tools and technology to serve as your guide to reconnecting with the past i.e. tracing your genealogy details.

Perhaps you have a rough idea about where your family came from or what they did; it could be enough to conduct an Internet search for lost relatives and kinsfolk scattered around different parts of the world. Besides the thrill of knowing the number of people connected to you by blood, you could maybe even find some new and interesting members of your family that can provide moral support and bonding in these tough, modern and complex times.

Get on the Net: sign up for free on the many genealogy websites to learn about your family, how they are linked to other families – even the kind of person you could be (quizzes and fun trivia by psychologists and sociologists exist on most of these that make for good reading).

At times, people consult genealogy websites for fun information or even some old heritage stuff that could possibly do them proud to discuss at gatherings; some may even do it for the sake of other family members (so they can reach out to a familiar face, long lost in the annals of time but found again thanks to technology). Goodness, imagine the thrill of finding out you are related to the radical and happening Martin Luther King Jr. or even Terrific Tee-offer, Tiger Woods! You'll surely be pleasantly surprised with uncanny connection to your family if you can establish a link with such personalities that are world renowned!

It would even be a good idea to look for traces of your family history if it has been long-forgotten down the ages and help others looking out for you and other family members to re-group in a joyous family reunion! Not only will you be reuniting long-lost but never-forgotten relatives, you may even be helping a brother find a sister and a re-married aunt find a loving grand-nephew! All that from simply getting on the net to search for family ancestry details, which is not at all difficult once you have the basic personal records right, such as date of birth, maiden name, married name or wedding details etc of the African Americans in your family tree! Isn't that great?

So, what are you waiting for? Its been over half a century since America's history was re-written by African American migrants from Africa who have contributed to every aspect of the country's development and progress – from education to economic prosperity to social reforms. Get online – and discover which branch of these great lives you spring from!

Methods of genealogical research- Valuable research tools for genealogy

Here are a few ideas and pointers which will help you in your research in genealogy.

Won't it be interesting to find out more information about your ancestral line several years back? The internet can be of good help if you are looking for reliable sources to help you as reference documents. It houses a lot of information to help you with your research. The best thing is effort and money is saved by the genealogist while using the internet for help.

Besides from knowing about their early background some may also want to know about their current generation. In this case genealogy becomes a quest and a serious study which involves a lot of investment.

You can also make use of some helpful tips that will make your research easier. Whether professional or not, it is important for you to understand that the chances of other people also working on your genealogy is more. Checking on the published work of people having your own surname involved in your family tree .Some researchers publish their work on the internet for others to visit it. Searchable indexes are some of the other tools found on the internet which help to find the information needed by your research.

You can also get help from the historical or genealogical society. They are normally found in the cities where your ancestors lived once. This is a great place to get to know about the time and life of your grandparents and great grandparents. The newspaper archives, the list of those buried in the inactive burial grounds, local directories all these are present in the historical or genealogical society. The plus point of this society is that it has volunteers who are in some way or other is related to genealogical facts. They even have the contact address of other such societies which are connected with their webs.

The Tradition of having cards for mourning or funerals was popular during the 1800's in Europe and the US. Genealogists find these cards as great sources of help. There are many websites which help people to index these cards. It is easy to search for and find surnames that you need by visiting these sites.

You can find a lot of local information from the newspapers. Valuable information about those who lived some years ago is available in these newspapers. The microfilm reels have been replaced by online newspaper archives which are searchable sites. Possessing information on your ancestors like events involving them will be helpful to you. While searching online, it is necessary to type the surname and the keyword which resembles the event. The information found in the online newspaper is reliable as it is regularly updated.

The index census can also be used for genealogical research. Beside there are some records which have been transcribed that can be obtained online. These records containing information on birth, marriage and death can be found in certain databases.

You can search your ancestry using the various tools available for research. There are sources which are provided only by proper organizations which are free and accessible.

Free Genealogy Database: A Great Way To Find Out About Your Ancestors

Finding about their family history is becoming more and more popular among many people today. Moreover this is something that can involve everyone at home. Try and find out about the history of your family, it will surely unfold a lot of mysteries and surprise you. For instance it has been found by the genealogists that, in politics, George W Bush is a distant cousin of John Kerry, his political opponent. It is surprising and funny when you notice that two cousins are battling it out for the most powerful place in America.

On researching the genealogy of your family you are sure to come upon many interesting and surprising facts. But one should also keep in mind that it is very costly to hire genealogists and they take their time to present to you a family tree which will have all the necessary information that you need to know about your relatives.

At present, thanks to the internet it is very easy and cheap to learn about the history of your family tree. There a few free genealogy websites which can help you in your quest. All that is required of you is to submit you name, birth date and country where you reside in and then click on the search button. This will help you know about your family tree in no time at all. But be careful, these kinds of free websites can provide you with inaccurate and unreliable results. A lot of hard work and time goes into tracing a family database. And so imagine the amount of work that would go into tracing millions of family trees. For even an experienced genealogist, it is a lot of hard work

The sites that you should visit first are genealogy database sites which are free of cost, if you have started your research on the family tree very recently. You will be able to find more different types of information on your family history which you can use later for accurate and comprehensive search .Spending money on important documents like birth, marriage, death and immigration records will be avoided

It is essential that you acknowledge the fact that these kinds of free genealogy searches are very basic and can provide you very limited information about the people with whom you are related. If you are looking for complete search on your history you will have to pay a certain amount for the information.

Suppose you have come to a dead end while searching on the free online sites, you can continue your search by looking through public records and old obituaries in the newspapers.

There are few things you should take into account while using free genealogy sites. Always keep in mind that the information obtained from these sites is very primitive. You can continue your search by looking through public library or you can hire experts and genealogist of good reputation to help you do the work, if your search online for the family tree has come to a stop .Give the genealogist the needed information as to how far you want to search to extend and the information that you collected from the preliminary research. These researches will know a lot about the documents and will also know where and how to search for it.

German Genealogy: Finding Your German Ancestors

United States is one of the countries in the world with a diverse culture and many believe that it is the "melting point" of the various different cultures and races in the world. Here you will see mixed races and culture. The country has people from all origins like from America, native America, Irish, Asian, British and German races too. Today there are over 300 million people who are living in the US.

At present the German Americans would be the biggest self reported cultural group in America. The census of 2000 reported that there is approximately 47million German Americans in the US. And so the possibility of you having a German background is greater. And if it happens to be true and provided you are interested, you can think about spending money to hire a genealogist to track your past.

Keep in mind that a chain of events in the world was responsible for the German people to move to America. It was the time period in-between 1680 to 1760 when the first American Germans moves to the US. After that the Germans formed the biggest group of Immigrants in America. The reason that they moved to the United States was the Conscription to the army, the deteriorating conditions to own a farm in their home land and the harassment of religious races.

They primarily choose the United States because of the freedom it offered them to own their farm lands and to practice any preferred religion and the absence of military conscription and most of all the better economy of America drew them towards this country.

Many German Jews, also migrated to America during the times of World War Two when Adolf Hitler came to the rule and began killing and persecuting them.

Therefore, it was a series of happening in the world which resulted in the Germans migrating to America. You will know that you have a German history if either you or you grand parents have an Aryan surnames. Tracing you ancestry can be quiet a task to complete. This is the reason as to why you should hire a genealogist to help you with the work. For all you know you may end up being related to some famous Germans like Oskar Schindler who saved millions of people ,especially Jews from the gas chambers of Adolf Hitler. Or you may also be related to the former president Dwight D Eisenhower or even to Albert Einstein.

How To Uncover Your Genealogy

There are many more Germans who are known to have made many contributions to the society. Actually Elvis Presley himself has a German origin.

Therefore you can consider the idea of hiring an expert to help you find your German history if and only if you are willing to find the lost German relatives of yours or the history of your family .With the improvement in technology it is very easy to track your German relatives.

Make The Best Use Of Genealogy Websites

When you are feeling that you life is missing something, try understanding your roots. And you can do so be studying or researching on genealogy. Collection of correct information from various sources can help your ancestors and this can be a smart way to begin your hunt. A genealogy website is the cheap way to look for information and it is sure to have abundant of information.

Internet has changed the face of tracking your ancestors. Years back, genealogy would have challenged us to do a lot of library work and travel long distances. In today's word there is a very effective tool called internet through which we can access free information. We should look to that proper care it taken to optimize the advantages of the genealogy websites as they are effective components of studying your genealogy. Accurate and reliable information are what you need in genealogy. Tutorial resource on genealogy will help the beginners as it will be a useful guide and the efforts gone into the work will not be wasted. The fundamental things that one should know to start with genealogy are the various types of documents and techniques.

Always document and remember the sources that you find on the free genealogy sites correctly. Indicate little information like the website address, notes and abbreviation at the index page or as foot notes. This will be very useful while checking the data that you have collected. At times the documentation may take the place of failing memory of the researcher. It is these documents which will help you solve some conflicting problems that you may come upon while researching.

The living relatives of yours can help to verify the data collected from the free genealogy sites. You can gather a good amount of information about your ancestors by interacting with them. Record the story along with the name of those who told it. And then you can compare and see if the information you have and their stories match together.

Death index, obituaries and census records are other sources on the net that can help your search. Although not all obituaries are published in the newspapers and not all newspapers publish the obituaries on the net, it can at least help and give you relative information and a little idea.

When you are done going over and collecting all the necessary information you will then have to organize the collected data. Highlight those documents and data that have the most value .At the same time do not discard those documents and data that are insignificant to you. These could help you for future reference.

Arranging the collected information is a hard works. But you can know that you are finished with the set once you reach this level. Interact with various other researchers and share the gathered facts. For all you know, it mite take more than just you to discover your history. "Two is better than one" is a saying and likely more than two are also good. For, you may not be the only one in your family who likes to find out more about your ancestors and heritage.

The Family History Library And International Genealogical Index

Searching for information on your genealogy can be difficult here is some information about two places which can possibly help you with your work.

The Church of Jesus Christ of LSD or the latter day saint has a family history library. This has more than 300,000 books, two million records in the form of microfilms and around 400,000 microfiche. Also there are a collection of manuscripts like indexes, family and local histories and other documents to help in genealogical research.

This library has a varied collection of information from different countries like China, Hungary, Chile and Netherlands. But more emphasis is given on countries like America, Europe, Great Britain and Canada. Using the archives the researchers can search for the original documents of the ancestors.

When it comes to the amount of information it holds from the United States, It has various documents from courthouses all around the country and regional and state records. The records containing the census of 1790 and 1920 are also present there.

This Family history library is very famous for its extensive knowledge and excellent assistance. One can get the staff's help to guide them throughout the search. Family Search computerized system and the loan programs between the libraries are other two main sources which are present in almost all the branches of this center all over world.

The International Genealogical Index (IGI)

Index record houses the birth and marriage records of all the people in its society, even of the dead. It originally begins by the submission of records by both the church members and others. In 1969 the Church of Latter saints started the IGI. And however the records dating to the time before 1970 were extracted. Improvement in the Extraction program was made just to prevent the people from getting documents from the church records. There are over hundred volunteers involved .They travel worldwide to film the documents. Then the other volunteers will transcribe these records on films

The Family History Library has come out with a list of records, The parish and vital records, which were extracted and listed in the IGI from almost all the geographical areas, the time periods and the new records .Usually the volunteers copy documents like .birth, death, marriages of the dead, the extraction of these records do not focus mainly on the ancestral lines of the members and the church volunteers.

The IGI has over 250 names listed in it. Most of the names are got from documents which date back to the time of 16th and 19th centauries. But at the same time not every name in the listed countries and those from the index documents are included in the IGI.

However, the names are not restrained to the people who are related to the members of the LSD .The IGI can be accessed anywhere from the Family history centers and library all around the country. Some of the genealogical centers and main libraries also have this facility. You can also access it through microfiche and CD-ROM.

Do not come to the false conclusion that all the records listed on IGI are accurate and taken from the original. There can always differ. And there is also a possibility that you may find incomplete records .At times the records may contain only dates and names. Those records which are complete were recorded before 1992.But never the less the Genealogical Index serves as a great and a vast source of information.

How Important Is Genealogy

Research on you family genealogy can be the answer to many of your questions.

You are here today in this world because of your ancestors whom you may have not seen before. Although both of you may have lead a very different life there may be a few similarities between both of you. One may be thinking why someone should learn about the people who are already dead. But when you come to know how important genealogy is, you will realize that it is challenging and fun, as said by some books.

Studying your family's genealogy you will discover and honor your ancestors and you will also find it interesting. It will help you learn many facts about your family, like why your parents grew from a place or other.

Foe example, way back in past, the American invaders have been fought by the Hessian soldiers who fought in the name of Great Britain. You may have relatives in Pennsylvania provided you find out that one of your family members was a Hessian soldier. Pennsylvania had a huge German-American population, mostly Hessian soldiers. But later they left for United States of America deserting the Great Britain. There they joined the American regime. Some of their descendants have settled in Ohio, so you can also search there.

At times you may wonder why a certain first name dominates almost the whole family tree, original surname before the American alterations. Most of the names are found difficult to pronounce by the immigrant officers. Therefore people change their surnames while undergoing the immigration process. From the ancestors livelihood you can discover the real surname. Mostly the surnames were obtained from the type of ancestor's occupation, for example, tanner, baker and so on.

Even medical condition are said to be passed on genetically from person to person. You can find out your medical histories once you find out your family's genealogy. You can find out more about the medical issues with cancer, auto immune disorder, and heart and so on and so forth. Mostly we come to know about the medical conditions through stories. Just in case you are not able to get any information, try searching the death notices which usually state the cause of the death. Therefore you will be able to take proper care of you and your health. Be more cautious of your eating, smoking and drinking habits if you happen to find out that cancer runs in your kin. This helps you to go through genetic tests.

If you are confused as to where to start with, books and research materials from the genealogy library or genealogy associations are the best way. Joining genealogy association and groups can also help you as they have research materials for you help. They also hold genealogy parties. You can also buy software and recently published books on genealogy. Internet is another source of help. Usually genealogy enthusiasts gather information from research materials and join forums to interact with far off relatives.

Where you get the information is not the question. It can be from the net or book or from other sources. No matter what, the goal is same, to discover the hidden past of your family by taking up the challenge.

Mormon Church Genealogy: Knowing About The History Of Mormons

Religion plays a very important role in a man's everyday activities. It acts as your moral guide and fills you with a sense of purpose. The movement of the Latter Day Saint which is also known as Mormon is a very famous religion t nowadays and it also belongs to Christianity.

However, the Mormon Church's genealogy is not very popular among the common people. Mormon is also considered to be adherents to the Latter Day Saints' Church of Jesus Christ. Referring to history, the word "Mormon" has been taken from the Book of Mormon. This religious book has been translated by a person called Joseph Smith, Jr. Information on the early American inhabitants' history has been compiled and written by a prophet named Mormon in this book.

Mormons are not members of the said religious sect, nor are they Protestants. They also do not take themselves to belong to the larger part of Christianity. At the same time, they also do not believe in Jesus Christ and what he represents.

The history of the Mormons is not very pleasant. They have undergone struggles and faced a lot of prosecution by various religions and sects of Christianity. The Mormon Book says that Prophet Mormon who dwelled in America in the fourth century heard God's call to compile information on his people and that too in the form of a single book

Right after Mormon died, his son who was called Moroni witnessed complete destruction and the persecution of his kind. It was him who hid the original version of the Mormon Book in upstate New York which was then a hill named Comorah.

It is said that Moroni had been a messenger whom God had sent to a person called Joseph Smith, Jr. Moroni then sent Smith to retrieve the book and translate it to the English language. Even though Smith did not know how to read or write the script of the book, he accurately and completely translated the Mormon Book. It was these miracles that have made Smith a prophet sent by God.

Yet, this was not the end of the struggles of the people of Mormons. In 1844, Smith was killed in a mob inside a Carthage at Illinois jail. Soon after that miserable year, many followers of the Saints of Latter-day started to follow Brigham Young who was chosen as the president in his denomination. After which he proceeded to Utah where he gave an Exodus to the Salt Lake City. This place now has the largest Mormon population in the world.

Till date, Mormon is a term which is used to refer to the group of people under Brigham Young in the Salt Lake City. However, other groups which are small have adopted the saints of Latter Day and are trying to reject using "Mormon" for describing their group. It was their claim that it did not make any reference to the central figure of their Church, that is the Mormon Church and the Church of the Saints of Latter Day.

The Mormons are completely different when it comes to theology, culture and practice among religious sects like Mennonites, Jehovah's witnesses, Amish and Society of Religious Friends. This is the Church of Mormon's genealogy. As is evident, Mormons are pretty different when compared to the other types of sects and Christian religion.

Steps On Finding Free Genealogy Information

Here are a few ideas to help you with you with the search on genealogy.

When it comes to researching on genealogy the information is very essential and important. There are a lot of sources which provide the necessary information, absolutely free of cost. But with the absence of guidelines, creating a research path is difficult. Finding genealogy information can be done in four steps.

1. **Collect the necessary information from the people you know and relatives.** This is a basic step in the research. While finding information, have a healthy cynicism. At times even the published records may have unrealistic status or legitimacy. At the same time it is not wise to think that all information which is published on the net is correct. Verify before using them.

2. **via internet get in touch with someone who mite knows about your family history.** These researches in genealogy require a lot of time and study. But try and make use of the internet, moreover it is easy and fast. To get connected and share information with other relatives and researchers, learn to use the message boards, email and email lists .And so you can identify online resources which are significant.

Always remember that you can get connected to other websites through web pages. Be sure that the sites you visit have associate programs .These is paid programs which can link you to other sites which can be useful in research. And there are a few sites which offer trial and offer subscriptions.

You can also try using the website which offers search capabilities using family or the surname. This links you automatically to other popular sites.

3. **Do the research using online databases which are free.** There are two main types of genealogy sites. Those which give you detailed information on papers and microfilms and explain the various ways of researching. And the other which give the online tools and searchable genealogy database.

But problems can be faced while working online. Both the small and the major websites may cause problems .Verification of the official records may not be finished. Or you may not be good at using the computer and the internet. Or the internet access may be slow. There is only one solution, be patient.

4.   Try not searching for meaningless records. It would be difficult to trace the history of your family if you do not have the correct information. Start the search from record indexes. Be sure to read the descriptions on the records. The place and time of census is important.

Use the images that you see on the transcribed information, provided you are making use of the internet technology. At time the images that you see on the record are done manually by someone. You can move information on the net once you read the real document. For instance, names of few people. Provide the original document as well as the names written clearly on the net. This way there is no difficulty in the comprehension of the illegible handwriting.

There is no need to worry since the sources are usually made easy using the new technology. The chances of a successful research are possible if you know how and what to do .Never loose your patience and give up hope even if it is difficult. Be sure that you have no regrets later in life.

The Family Tree

Ho one is related to another is the first question that very one asks when in a family gathering. Usually people start to identify a person's connection to the "family circle". The family lineage helps a person to identify the relationship between each person in the family.

To emphasis on the relationship between the relatives, make sure to include a few important facts in the family tree:

- Person's name
- Birth date
- And other information likes employment and physical address

You should also distinguish the relationship by

1. Marriage
2. Extra marital unions
3. Progeniture

When you are doing your own family tree, then there is not much of trouble. But when it comes to finding the family tree involving your ancestors, a lot of time has to be spent to familiarize yourself with the roots.

A clear understanding of your family lineage is needed and you need to find out correctly about the history of your ancestors if you want form a complete family tree

It is because of a pair that the family has started. However the genealogy study shows that any kind of problem in the family tree would be due to two main bases.

The first main complication will arise in the family when the man has more than one wife. Identifying such family trees will be very difficult since there would be many family lines to trace.

How To Uncover Your Genealogy

A large family is another source of family complexity .But on the bright side it is very helpful when it comes to genealogy. The smaller the family the sooner you will be able to finish tracing your family tree.

It will be the time to begin your task once you find out the type of family arrangement that you have. Start with your task of completing a well designed and researched family tree.

Always starts from the basics. From the older family members you can obtain information about your ancestors and roots. They can help by giving you clues on where to start your next search.

Every meeting with your relatives must be documented. Tape recorders, video cams or journals or cameras can be handy. Fill out all the relevant data in your genealogical form or in the family tree. Due to the availability of several family trees in the market you don't have to sketch your own.

You will come by many surnames through your journey for completing a family tree. It is advisable to choose the surname that you find first in lineage. You are sure to finish the work faster if you focus on the surname. Once you find out all the information on a particular surname and you feel that the search is complete, you can then move ob to the other surname.

Sometimes it may not be enough to just interview your family members. Through other sources like internet, documents like birth, death and marriage certificates, family history center and places like court house, church and even cemetery you can find out your relatives.

To help you know you own identity and roots, a family tree is very important.

Role Of DNA Testing In Genealogy Research

The human body has over 60.00 cells. White blood cells Cheek and muscle cells are also included in this. Deoxyribonucleic acid (DNA) information is present in each of these cell structures. The autosomal DNA, X chromosomal DNA and Y chromosomal DNA or just the DNA is present inside the cell's nucleus. Mitochondrial DNA (mtDNA) is held in the nucleus's outer part. Both the father and mother contribute for the autosomal DNA .A son inherits the Y chromosome from his father while the mother is responsible for the mtDNA.

Many improvements have been made in DNA research to help the various fields. For instance, they are used to prove the paternity or to find criminals. Nowadays even genealogy researches take the help of DNA testing.

For the last few years, genealogy research has evolved to become a major part of the society and the much preferred hobby of enthusiasts. But at time this can frustrate even the expert genealogists no matter how rewarding it may be. Paper research in this field can be time consuming work. Very often it leads to damaged documents and illegible handwriting. DNA testing gives instant results and there is no need to doubt its quality or authenticity. And at the same time the results of genetic genealogy can stand against the test of time.

1.   **The maternal background of a person can be traced by mitochondrial testing.** This is very important because when it comes to mtDNA testing the genealogists are normally females. Their maternal lines are usually lost because of the change in surname after marriage. With the help of this it will be easier for them to learn about their maternal background.

Many improvements have been made in making genetics easier to understand and in using the lab techniques to help someone find their maternal line using mtDNA tracing. The lost ancestry l line can be found out by testing the mtDNA of the person and comparing it with the database of mtDNA samples.

Even after many years the mtDNA remains unchanged. You may share the exactly same mtDNA with your mother, grandmother and great-grandmother) .Using the mtDNA code you can track your maternal heritage right from the place where the first mutation of your mtDNA occurred.

Through mitochondrial eve or by natural mutation, today, women can retrace their origin 150,000 years ago. The common ancestor is eve in association with matrilineal descent. This doest not mean that the only women who lived during that era were eve. There were many other women. But it was only eve's lineage which survived.

2. **the most commonly used form of testing in respect to genetic genealogy is the Y chromosomal DNA testing.** You can even find out if you are related to a deceased man through this test.

Just like mtDNA the Y chromosomes are traced right from its father, Adam. The first DNA mutation of Y chromosomes occurred over many years. Your paternal line can be traced by comparing your Y chromosomes with those available worldwide Y database.

Genealogists can also find out the relation between two people if they have the same surnames. This possible since in almost all cultures the children inherit the surname from the father just like they inherit Y chromosomal DNA

DNA testing is very essential in making the genealogy test successful as it has proven to be very helpful in the last few years.

This Product Is Brought To You By

www.ingramcontent.com/pod-product-compliance
Lightning Source LLC
LaVergne TN
LVHW012126070526
838202LV00056B/5880